WE LOVE CALIFORNIA

BY GABRIELLA FRANCINE

WITH SOLARA VAYANIAN   •   ILLUSTRATED BY PHIL VELIKAN

BBM BOOKS
Newport Beach, CA

For Oprah Winfrey, for inspiring me to take a chance on my dream.

To learn more about the great state of California, we recommend visiting the following great websites:
For information about the Golden Gate Bridge, visit it's official website, www.goldengatebridge.org.
For information about the state flag, visit www.bearflagmuseum.org.
To learn about the official state marine mammal, the gray whale, visit any of the following:
The Gray Whale Foundation www.graywhalefoundation.org, www.savethewhales.org,
www.journeynorth.org, and www.graywhalescount.org.

To learn more about how to fight hunger in California and throughout the world, visit these websites:
Feeding America: Hunger in America www.feedingamerica.org
The California Association of Food Banks www.cafoodbanks.org
The Food Bank of Contra Costa and Solano www.foodbankccs.org
Second Harvest Food Bank of Orange County www.feedoc.org

Layout, cover and illustrations by Phil Velikan www.findphil.com • Illustrations created in watercolor and pencil
Photography by Holly Kondras
Editorial assistance provided by Dorothy Chambers
Packaged by Wish Publishing

Printed in China
10 9 8 7 6 5 4 3 2 1

Published by BBM Books

Special thanks to Wish Publishing for their help bringing this book into being
and to Claire Willey and Lexi Zelensky for their roles in the journey.

"Are you ready, Avery?" says Olivia. "This will be a great adventure!"
"Are we really going to collect all of the symbols of the State of California?" asks Avery.
"Yes! You can be the navigator — and hold the flag up high!"

"Oh!" says Avery. "It's kind of dark in here. Are you sure you know where we're going?"

"Yes. These are the giant Sequoias, the California state tree. They must be five miles high!"

Olivia looks over at Avery. "Are you scared?"

"Um, no."

"Singing will make you less scared – let me teach you the California state song!"

"I like that! And I do feel braver now!"

STATE TREE

I Love You, California

Written by F. B. Silverwood • Composed by A. F. Frankenstein

I love you, California, you're the greatest state of all
I love you in the winter, summer, spring, and in the fall.
I love your fertile valleys; your dear mountains I adore,
I love your grand old ocean and I love her rugged shore.

Chorus
Where the snow crowned Golden Sierras
Keep their watch o'er the valleys bloom.
It is there I would be in our land by the sea,
Ev'ry breeze bearing rich perfume.
It is here nature gives of her rarest,
It is Home Sweet Home to me.
And I know when I die I shall breathe my last sigh
For my sunny California.

I love your redwood forests - love your fields of yellow grain.
I love your summer breezes, and I love your winter rain.
I love you, land of flowers; land of honey, fruit and wine.
I love you, California; you have won this heart of mine.

Chorus

I love your old gray Missions - love your vineyards stretching far.
I love you, California, with your Golden Gate ajar.
I love your purple sunsets, love your skies of azure blue.
I love you, California; I just can't help loving you.

Chorus

I love you, Catalina - you are very dear to me.
I love you, Tamalpais, and I love Yosemite.
I love you, Land of Sunshine, half your beauties are untold.
I loved you in my childhood, and I'll love you when I'm old.

STATE SONG

3

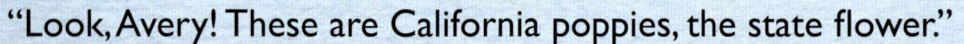

"Look, Avery! These are California poppies, the state flower."
"There are millions of them!" cries Olivia. "What a beautiful golden color."
"They look like little cups of gold."

STATE FLOWER

"Olivia! A - a - a bear!!" screams Avery, pointing.
"Hi, girls, I'm Cuffy the Grizzly - the California state bear. See?
I look just like the bear on the flag. He's my great, great, great, great uncle."
"Are you going to eat us?" asks Avery.
Cuffy laughs. "No, no. I'm here to help you find your California symbols.
I bet we can find another California symbol over in that river!"

STATE BEAR

"Look, it's a Golden Trout, the California state fish. Isn't he beautiful?"
"Oh, yes!"

STATE FISH

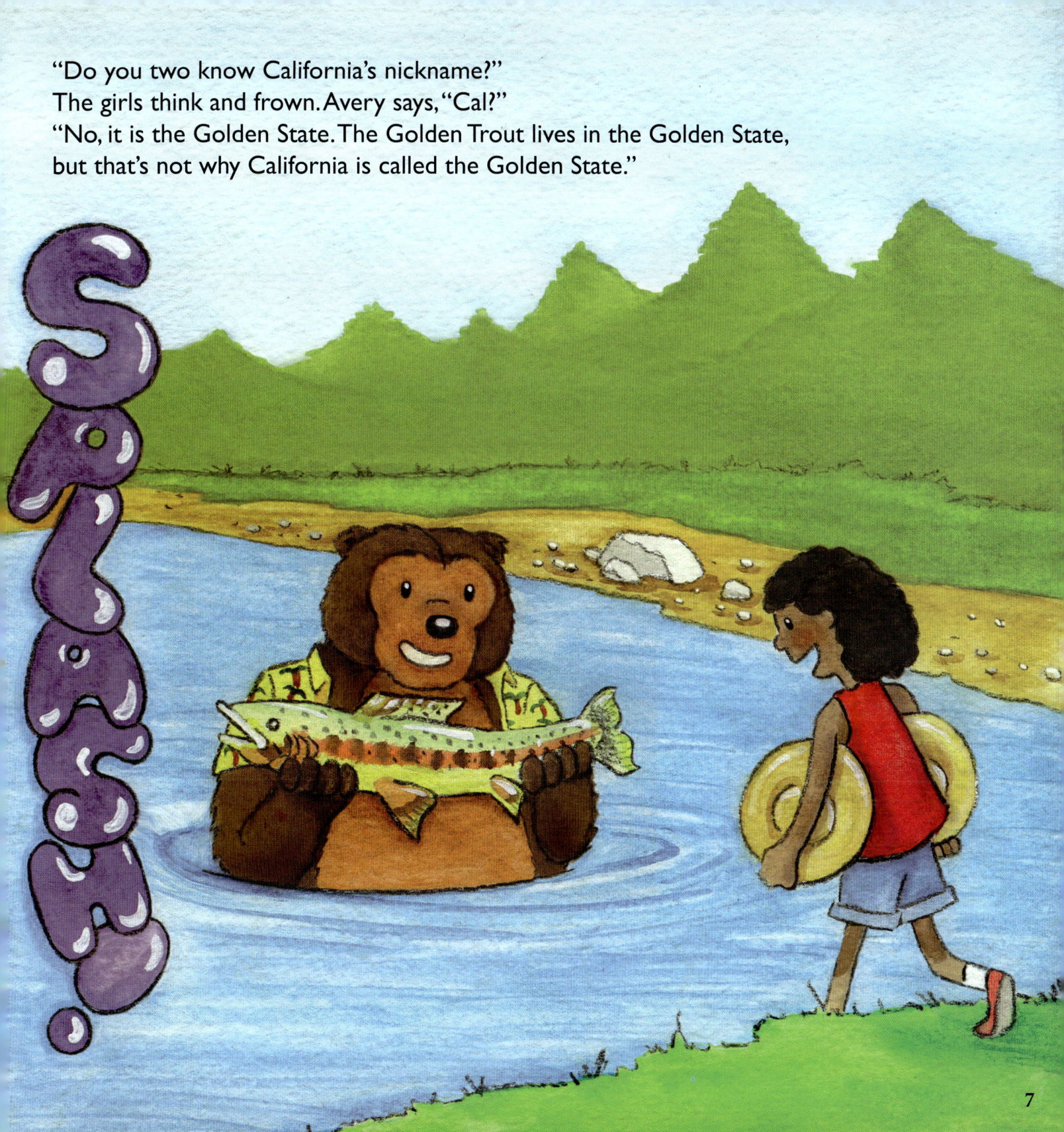

"Do you two know California's nickname?"
The girls think and frown. Avery says, "Cal?"
"No, it is the Golden State. The Golden Trout lives in the Golden State,
but that's not why California is called the Golden State."

"The real reason California is called the Golden State started here on the American River in Coloma. Back in 1848, a carpenter who was building a sawmill discovered gold."
"Wow! Real gold?" says Olivia.
"Yes, real gold. People came from all over the world because they hoped to become rich."
"Did they get rich?" wonders Avery.
"A few," answers Cuffy. "Most didn't. It's hard to dig for gold. But it made California famous."

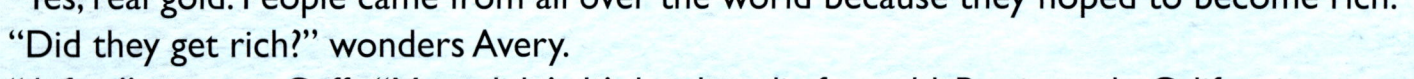

"Look, here's another symbol of California, girls. Do you know the name of the lovely grass we see growing here?" says Cuffy.

"Is it Purple Needlegrass?" asks Olivia. "I've seen it growing by my grandpa's farm."

"Yes, it is the official state grass of California," says Cuffy. "Here, smell it, Avery. Now let's head for Sacramento and the state capital!"

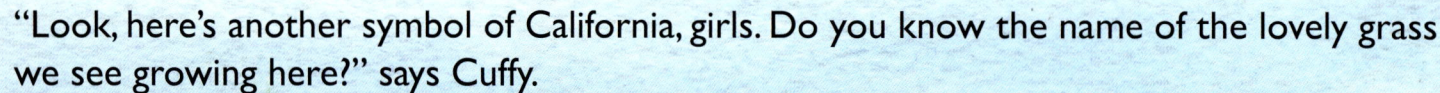
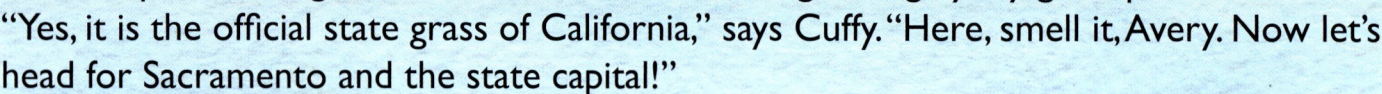

STATE GRASS

10

"This is the capitol building for the whole state of California?" asks Avery.

"Yes, indeedy," answers Cuffy.

"It's very nice. But why do they have that big sign saying *Find Yourself Here*? I find myself wherever I am," says Olivia.

"That is the California state slogan. And *Eureka* is the state motto."

FIND YOURSELF HERE!

STATE CAPITOL

"And this is the California seal, girls!" states Cuffy.
"There is that word *Eureka* right inside the seal," says Olivia. "But what does that mean?"

STATE SEAL

"I found it!" yells Cuffy.

Avery asks, "You found what?"

"Eureka. Eureka means 'I found it.' It's what the miners yelled when they found gold."

Olivia thinks for a minute. "So in California, I find it, and I find myself."

"That's about the size of it," laughs Cuffy.

"Let's stop in that museum," says Olivia. "I want to see if they have any fossils or pictures of the Saber-Toothed Tiger."
"Is that the state tiger?" asks Avery.
Cuffy laughs. "Not anymore! They lived thousands of years ago. Today their bones are the California state fossil."

"What is a fossil, exactly?" asks Avery.

"Bones," answers Olivia. "Bones of something that lived a long time ago. When the animal died, the bones got covered with dirt or laid in a cave or something until somebody found them many years later."

"The bones tell us what the animal looked like," adds Cuffy.

STATE FOSSIL

"Cuffy, these are so beautiful! What are they?" says Olivia.
"They look like blue diamonds!" adds Avery.
"They are called blue diamonds," says Cuffy.
"Their real name is Benitoite. They are the
California state gemstone."

CALIFORNIA DANCE FESTIVAL

STATE GEMSTONE

"Cuffy," laughs Olivia, "you're a really good dancer. Do you know all the steps?"
"Of course! I have to know all the steps. The West Coast Swing is the California state dance, and I am the California state bear!"

STATE DANCE

"History in action!" exclaims Cuffy.
"This is the California state folk dance. Do you know what it is?"
"The Lumber Jack?" guesses Avery.
"No, it's the Square Dance!" Cuffy says, bouncing up and down.
"Let me show you before we leave."

STATE FOLK DANCE

"Hey look! The California state insect!"
"What are they?" asks Avery.
"The California Dogface Butterfly, am I right?" says Olivia proudly.
"Yes," says Cuffy. "See how the wings of some of them look like dog faces?"
"But why only some?" wonders Avery.
"Just the males have dog faces," answers Cuffy, "just the males."

STATE INSECT

STATE DRINK

20

"Yummmmm… Look at these!" says Cuffy. "Not only are they good to eat, but they are also made into the California state drink."

"Is it soda pop?" asks Avery.

"No, guess again. It comes in lovely bottles and can be red or white, pink or kind of golden."

"Hot chocolate?" asks Olivia.

"Oh, you're too young. Don't your parents drink wine?" asks Cuffy.

"Oh, yes!" smiles Olivia. "Wine."

"California is famous for its wine, and the grapes grow in some of our valleys, like the Napa Valley."

"This is America's salad bowl, the San Joaquin Valley," says Cuffy.

"Salad bowl?" cry both girls together. "How can it be a salad bowl?"

"It is called a salad bowl because there are many farms here growing food for our nation."

"Oh," says Olivia. "So salad grows here."

"Yes, I suppose you could say that. It grows in the rich soil of the valley, the San Joaquin soil, California's official state soil."

STATE SOIL

23

"Look at these beautiful birds," says Olivia.
"Yes, California Valley Quail, our state bird."

STATE BIRD

"And here is the California state reptile — the Desert Tortoise," says Olivia.
"He's lived here for 100 years and can go up to one full year without a drink of water."
"Wow," says Avery. "How can he do that?"
"His body actually stores water."
"I wish my body stored water," says Avery.

STATE REPTILE

STATE MARINE
MAMMAL

26

"The ocean is so huge!" exclaims Avery.
"What's that over there, coming out of the water, Cuffy?"
"Girls, what a privilege! The Gray Whale, the California state marine mammal, is making an appearance just for us!"
"Ohh, he's beautiful and so BIG!"
"Yes. Gray Whales grow to become 35 to 50 feet long. And they weigh between 20 and 40 tons!"

"Do you see those tall ships?" asks Cuffy. "These are called schooners. People looking for gold arrived in them. They are the California state tall ship."

STATE SHIP

"Oh, Cuffy, I think I hear my mother calling me," says Olivia. "It's a good thing we have already found so many of California's symbols."
"Well, it sure took long enough," says Avery.

"That was a wonderful adventure!"